SCHOOL INSPECTION
IN ENGLAND:
A RE-APPRAISAL

PREVIOUSLY PUBLISHED IN THE IMPACT SERIES

IMPACT 1   Andrew Davis
             Educational Assessment: a critique of current policy
             October 1999

IMPACT 2   Michael Luntley
             *Performance, Pay and Professionals: measuring the
             quality of teaching - a challenge to the government's
             proposals on teachers' pay*
             January 2000

IMPACT 3   Harry Brighouse
             Educational Equality and the New Selective Schooling
             January 2000

IMPACT 4   Christopher Winch
             New Labour and the Future of Training
             February 2000

IMPACT 5   Kevin Williams
             *Why Teach Foreign Languages in Schools?
             A challenge to government policy*
             June 2000

IMPACT 6   Steve Bramall and John White
             Will the new National Curriculum live up to its aims?
             June 2000

IMPACT 7   David Archard
             Sex Education
             September 2000

IMPACT 8   Stephen Johnson
             Teaching Thinking Skills
             July 2001

Impact No.9

School Inspection in England: A Re-Appraisal

BY COLIN RICHARDS

Edited by Christopher Winch and Richard Smith

Published by the Philosophy of Education Society of Great Britain

First published in 2001 by the
Philosophy of Education Society of Great Britain

©Philosophy of Education Society of Great Britain

Distributed by Business and
Medical Book Centre
9 Headlands Business Park
Ringwood, Hants BH24 3PB

British Library Cataloguing in Publication Data:
a catalogue record for this publication is available
in the British Library

ISBN 0-902227-09-2

Printed by Formara Limited
16 The Candlemakers,
Temple Farm Industrial Estate,
Southend on Sea, Essex SS2 5RX

CONTENTS

page

Editorial introduction   vii

Overview   1

Introduction   5

1   What is inspection?   8

2.   Aims, values and inspection   10

3.   The language of inspection   14

4.   The inspection of standards   18

5.   The inspection of teaching and learning   27

6.   More limitations of inspection   36

7.   Conclusion: possibilities for inspection   41

Notes   44

References   45

Suggestions for further reading   47

THE IMPACT
EDITORIAL TEAM

EDITORIAL INTRODUCTION

This is the ninth IMPACT pamphlet. IMPACT is an initiative of the Philosophy of Education Society of Great Britain. Its purpose is to bring philosophical perspectives to bear on current UK education policy.

The IMPACT series was launched in late 1999. Its papers have been commissioned from leading general philosophers and philosophers of education interested in exploring the assumptions behind current policy.

IMPACT pamphlets have covered a wide range of government policies: assessment in schools, performance-related pay for teachers, allocation to secondary education, post-16 training policy, the place of foreign languages in the curriculum, the aims of the school curriculum after 2000, sex education. Sometimes they have focused on controversial aspects of on-going policy, such as those by Andrew Davis on assessment or Harry Brighouse's on disparities in secondary education. Sometimes they have tackled a new policy initiative, as with Michael Luntley's critique of performance-related pay, Chris Winch's discussion of the 1999 White Paper *Learning to Succeed*, Kevin Williams's paper on foreign language teaching in schools, published in the same week as the Nuffield Report *Languages - the Next Generation*, and Steve Bramall and John White's commentary on the relation between the aims of the post-2000 school curriculum and the curriculum itself.

Each IMPACT paper has been accompanied by a symposium for policy - makers and others at which the issues raised have been further explored. The new pamphlets have clearly succeeded in their purpose of showing policy-makers how useful philosophy can be in testing the credentials of current initiatives and suggesting how they can be improved. IMPACT symposia have attracted Government Ministers and their opposition Shadows, other members of parliament, chief executives from a wide range of organisations including the Qualifications and Curriculum Authority, the Institute of Directors, the Trades Union Congress, the General Teaching Council, the National Union of Teachers, Politeia and Demos, as well as educational journalists and academics involved in policy-making.

Further IMPACT papers are being published at the rate of roughly two per year. The next ones will cover government initiatives on citizenship education and on personal, social and health education. A full list of topics due to appear over the next year can be found at the end of this pamphlet.

Also at the end of every pamphlet, including this one, there is a list of suggestions for further reading. This enables readers to examine opposing, or simply alternative, arguments on the same issues.

Each IMPACT pamphlet expresses the ideas of its author or authors only. It does not represent the view of the Philosophy of Education Society of Great Britain. There is, indeed, no such single view. PESGB contains several hundred members whose ideas and political allegiances are widely disparate.

The topicality and importance of the IMPACT series is well illustrated by Colin Richards' pamphlet on *School Inspection*. The regime under which schools (and, in future, Colleges of Further Education) are inspected by the Office for Standards in Education has of course been highly controversial. It has been a key element in the Government's campaign to raise educational standards. At the same time it has been accused of playing a major part in demoralising the teaching profession, of measuring only those things that can easily be measured, and so of damaging our sense of the richness of education and its possibilities.

Among the extreme claims made both against and behalf of Ofsted's regime of school inspection Colin Richards' pamphlet achieves a critical but carefully reasoned tone. He argues that this regime promises more than it can possibly deliver, and that there is a wide and unacknowledged element of subjective judgement in school inspection. He argues too that Ofsted has no coherent and defensible *theory* of what it does. This last point is particularly ironic in view of the widespread emphasis on accountability in education: if those who hold schools to account cannot give a proper account of their own practice, then something does indeed seem to have gone wrong.

Colin Richards sees a continuing and important role for Ofsted, or for some successor inspection regime, but only after its whole process, values and methodology have been subjected to the radical review that this pamphlet argues they urgently need.

Colin Richards was formerly one of Her Majesty's Inspectors of Schools, and is now Professor of Education at St. Martin's College, Cumbria.

Overview

The Office for Standards in Education (Ofsted) was created almost ten years ago as an instrument of accountability through the 1992 Education Act. The second and more controversial of its chief inspectors resigned late in 2000. The time is propitious for a re-appraisal of the Ofsted system of inspection.

Summed up very briefly, my argument is that the Ofsted inspection system promises more than it can deliver. It claims more than it can justifiably claim. Its judgements are inevitably more partial and subjective than it acknowledges.

Inspection and aims

Ofsted employs inspectors to *inspect* schools but what is the nature of inspection? Ofsted never satisfactorily addresses this basic issue. I argue that inspection involves more than observing, gathering evidence and reporting it orally or in writing. Inspectors are not simply a human form of camera, neutrally capturing what goes on in schools. They have to make *judgements*, not measurements; they have to interpret, not just record; they have to make judgements about whether what they are observing or scrutinising is *worthwhile;* they can only make those judgements against a background of aims and values. But what are those aims and values? Ofsted is silent on such issues. Its inspectors should not make such overall judgements about 'effectiveness' or 'quality' in the absence of explicit aims and values. When and because they do so, Ofsted promises more than it can deliver.

Inspection language

Quite rightly, Ofsted expects its inspectors to report using 'everyday language' but people use and understand words in different ways. This means that Ofsted reports are never, and can never be, absolutely clear, precise or unambiguous; they are inevitably going to be interpreted in different ways by different people. The judgements they report in 'everyday language'are at best inspectors' professional judgements, inevitably value-laden and inevitably subjective to a degree. Readers of inspection reports (and Ofsted itself !) need to be aware of the danger of treating inspection judgements as more definitive or precise than they can possibly be.

Inspection of standards

Strictly speaking, 'standards' are benchmarks or norms against which the quality of a particular activity or process is evaluated. Strictly speaking, Ofsted does not report on such 'standards' but on schools' or pupils' performance in relation to them. The standards of pupils' attainment reported by Ofsted are embodied in National Curriculum level descriptions or in GCSE and A/AS grade descriptors. These are contentious: not every one agrees on their worth or appropriateness. Also, since they are expressed in everyday language, they can be, and will be, interpreted somewhat differently by inspectors and the teachers being inspected in a particular school. This does not mean that inspectors cannot or should not make judgements in relation to level or grade descriptions but it does mean that they should do so only in a rough-and-ready, tentative way and that their judgements may quite properly be challenged by teachers whose work is being inspected.

When reporting standards Ofsted gives priority to the reporting of performance data, particularly in the Core subjects in Key Stages 1-3. Ofsted's uncritical use of performance data fails to acknowledge that there are fundamental disagreements over their reliability, their validity and the uses to which they are put. Tellingly, Ofsted places far more emphasis on performance data as so-called 'measures' of standards than it does on the judgements of its own registered and team inspectors.

Again, in reporting on standards of attainment Ofsted promises more than it can deliver. Its reporting is partial, potentially flawed and far from incontrovertible or uncontentious.

Inspection of teaching and learning

Ofsted makes much of its claim to be able to evaluate 'the quality of teaching, judged in terms of its impact on pupils' learning and what makes it successful or not'. In reality there are considerable limitations on its inspectors' ability to make such judgements.

In relation to learning inspectors are limited largely to commenting on pupils' *observable* responses. They can comment, for example, on whether pupils appear interested, whether they seem to be concentrating on their work, whether they actively contribute to a lesson, and so on. I argue that except in a minority of cases inspectors cannot assess the extent of children's learning in lessons

Inspectors' ability to judge the 'impact' of teaching on learning is equally limited. Except in certain cases inspectors cannot evaluate the effectiveness of teaching in bringing about learning in the lessons they observe. Inspectors can, however, comment legitimately and valuably on the way lessons are conducted. What inspectors appear to be doing increasingly is judging how far the lessons they see conform to 'accepted' models of 'good' teaching promulgated by central government. But 'good' in this sense does not *necessarily* mean 'good' in the sense of *enhancing children's learning*.

As before, Ofsted claims too much when it makes strong, unequivocal statements about the quality of teaching and learning in schools nationally or in particular schools.

Inspection of progress and improvement

I also argue that Ofsted inspectors are not in a position to evaluate and report on pupils' progress either in particular lessons or over longer periods of time and therefore cannot comment on schools' contribution to that progress. Likewise they cannot evaluate the extent of a school's improvement from one inspection to the next. The necessary evidence and other conditions to make valid comparisons and judgements of improvement are simply not available. Again Ofsted promises too much and schools may be judged unfairly as a result.

Possibilities

Assuming at least some of my arguments are sound, where does that leave Ofsted inspection? Should the Ofsted inspection process be modified, be radically overhauled or be dispensed with altogether? Certainly the limitations I have outlined imply that the Ofsted process is in need of urgent review.

I go on to suggest eleven uses for school inspection which take account of the criticisms I have raised. I believe these to be valuable in informing educational policy and practice but they are much more limited than the claims Ofsted itself makes for inspection.

Introduction

The Office for Standards in Education (Ofsted) has been in operation since 1992. Through the inspection system which it regulates, it

- holds all state schools accountable to central and local government and to parents for the educational standards and quality of education they achieve;

- provides information about standards and quality to inform parental choice of schools;

- ensures that schools comply with government legislation and regulations;

- provides evidence of schools' value for money in terms of educational benefits as against costs.

It is one of a number of instruments of accountability set up by central government in the UK in the last decade or so of the twentieth century. Others have included the establishment of the Audit Commission (with a remit including, but wider than, education), the enlargement of the powers of school governing bodies, the requirement laid on local authorities to monitor school performance, the introduction of national testing of selected outcomes of schooling and the publication of performance or 'league tables'.[1] Unlike other instruments of accountability Ofsted evaluates and reports not just the outcomes of education in individual schools but also the quality of the processes and activities employed in them. It also seeks out and reports on inter-relationships or associations between processes and outcomes, based largely on first-hand evidence gathered as a result of observation and discussion with teachers and pupils.

Its main operational task has been to oversee the introduction and regulation of a new system of school inspection by independent inspectors so that over a limited period (initially four years, now six) every maintained school in England has a full inspection lasting several days, involving a number of inspectors who use a publicly available inspection framework and methodology including pre-determined inspection criteria. These inspections are intended 'to identify strengths and weaknesses so that schools may improve the quality of education they provide and raise the educational standards achieved by their pupils' (Ofsted 1995). The programme of national inspections has been carried out by independent inspectors under contract to inspection agencies (such as commercial organisations or local education authority services) who are themselves under contract to Ofsted. As far as most teachers, parents, politicians and the general public are concerned school inspection has come to be identified with full inspections carried out by Ofsted inspectors working to Ofsted criteria.

Ofsted inspection has been the subject of great controversy since 1992, in terms of its purposes, its methodology, the expertise of its inspectors, its contracting procedures, the use of its results by Her Majesty's Chief Inspector (HMCI) and others and particularly in terms of its effects on schools and individual teachers. In this pamphlet I am not primarily concerned with the effects of Ofsted inspection on schools, teachers and the education service.[2] Instead I am trying to establish some of the limitations, as well as some of the possibilities, of Ofsted inspection in particular and of inspection in general. My main points are illustrated largely by reference to the inspection of primary schools (of which I have some experience) but they are also applicable, I believe, to the inspection of secondary and special schools, and, with modifications, to the inspection of initial teacher education and training.

1
What is inspection?

Nowhere in current official documentation is the nature of inspection spelt out. The duties and responsiblities of Ofsted are described in a number of publications. Commentators have analysed what they see as the functions served by Ofsted inspection, such as to hold schools accountable, to provide information to aid parental choice, to ensure compliance with government directives and to provide evidence of value for money. However, quite what inspection *is* is never considered, but presupposed.

Perhaps to refer to the legal framework under which Ofsted operates might help in elucidating what inspection is. Currently, school inspection is governed by the School Inspections Act 1996.

Section 10 of that Act says that registered inspectors must report on

- the educational standards achieved in the school;

- the quality of education provided by the school;

- whether the financial resources made available to the school are managed efficiently;

- the spiritual, moral, social and cultural development of pupils at the school. (Ofsted 1999a p. 4)

Presumably then inspection involves at the very least the collection and reporting of evidence on 'educational standards', on 'quality', on 'efficient management of resources' and on the four strands of pupils' 'development'. But what counts as evidence of 'standards', 'quality' or 'development'? Can such evidence be provided without a judgement as to what counts as 'standards' or 'quality'? And is the provision of evidence sufficient? Doesn't inspection also involve elements of interpretation and normative judgement in relation to the evidence presented?

As a process inspection involves more than observing, collecting evidence and reporting it. Inspectors are not simply the equivalent of value-free cameras or video-recorders providing snap-shots of schools and classrooms. Inspection involves the *interpretation*, not just the *reporting*, of activities. Crucially, too, it involves making judgements as to the worthwhileness of what is observed, collected and reported. It involves the making (and justification) of qualitative judgements; such judgements are inevitably subjective to a degree since they involve both the interpretation of complex social situations and the application of general criteria expressed in 'everyday language' (see pp. 14 - 17). To be valid interpretations such judgements need to be informed by an understanding of the aims and values of the activity or organisation being inspected and of how these relate to the aims and values of the educational system itself.

Many of the aspects of schools on which Ofsted inspection reports are value-laden and contentious: 'quality', 'value for money', 'best strategic use of resources', 'best value', 'improvement' are obvious examples. Other less evident ones include 'standards', 'effectiveness', 'strengths' and 'weaknesses'. To take a simple example, should sport be considered one of a school's 'strengths' if its teams regularly win inter-school competitions but sport assumes a disproportionate importance in pupils' eyes? It all depends on what you think a school is *for*, or what your vision of educational values is. Nowhere does Ofsted recognise the value-ladenness of many of the key terms it uses.

2
Aims, values and inspection

What are, or should be, the aims and values employed in inspection when making judgements as to the worthwhileness of the activities of schools, teachers and pupils? Ofsted documentation does not deal with this question at all.

This is not surprising since the English educational system has long lacked a *detailed* statement of the aims and values which should underpin and inform its activities, including the activities involved in inspection. Not until very recently has any such statement been produced. We do however now have the statement of the values, purposes and aims underlying the school curriculum published in the National Curriculum handbooks for primary and secondary teachers in England (DfEE/QCA 1999a, b). Surprisingly, given its importance, the statement is neither statutory nor mandatory in state schools. It has not been shaped, as it might and perhaps should have been, as a result of a thorough nationwide consultation involving all or even a substantial number of teachers. It is incomplete, focusing as it does on the school *curriculum* rather than on the *education* provided in schools. Some of its phrases are loosely worded and subject to diverse interpretation. But even so, as Bramall and White point out, it 'presents a coherent, humane vision by which schools [and, I would add, the inspection of schools] can be guided' (Bramall and White 2000, p. 14). It is certainly a major step forward in elucidating the aims of school education in England.

The values underpinning the school curriculum are made very clear in the opening paragraphs of the handbooks (DfEE/QCA 1999a, b, p. 10):

Foremost is a belief in education, at home and at school, as a route to the spiritual, moral, social, cultural, physical and mental development, and thus the well-being, of the individual. Education is also a route to equality of opportunity for all, a healthy and just democracy, a productive economy, and sustainable development. Education should reflect the enduring values that contribute to these ends. These include valuing ourselves, our families and other relationships, the wider groups to which we belong, the diversity in our society and the environment in which we live. Education should also reaffirm our commitment to the virtues of truth, justice, honesty, trust and a sense of duty.

At the same time education must enable us to respond positively to the opportunities and challenges of the rapidly changing world in which we live and work. In particular, we need to be prepared to engage as individuals, parents, workers and citizens with economic, social and cultural change, including the continued globalisation of the economy and society, with new work and leisure patterns and with the rapid expansion of communication technologies.

These values underpin two broad aims (*ibid.*, p. 11):

Aim 1: The school curriculum should aim to provide opportunities for all pupils to learn and to achieve...

Aim 2: The school curriculum should aim to promote pupils' spiritual, moral, social and cultural development and prepare all pupils for the opportunities, responsibilities and experiences of life.

From these broad goals are derived a considerable number of determinate aims intermediate in scope between the two broad 'aims' above and a large number of more specific objectives.[3] Such aims include, for example, that the curriculum should enable pupils to think creatively and critically, that it should encourage them to recognise the importance of pursuing a healthy lifestyle, and that it should promote equal opportunities and enable pupils to challenge discrimination and stereotyping *(ibid.)*.

As will be discussed later, such aims are inevitably open to interpretation but less so than the very general, vague and grandiose aims that feature, for example in the Education Reform Act of 1988 or the DES publication *Better Schools* (1985).

If these do represent at least some of the determinate aims which the English education system deems important and which primary, secondary and special schools are trying to achieve, then school inspection involves:

- gathering evidence about a school's activities;
- interpreting that evidence in the light of these aims and values;
- evaluating that evidence through judging the *worthwhileness* of the activities in fostering those commonly agreed aims and in embodying those values;
- reporting those judgements.

Currently the Ofsted inspection process involves collecting, evaluating and reporting evidence but without any explicit reference to aims or values. Unless they are tied into explicit values or aims, judgements that x and y are of 'good quality' mean nothing, apart from conveying a general sense of approval together with a wholly erroneous implication that x and y have passed tests of quality control like a computer or microwave and are thus of good quality in a more objective sense. Judgements of the 'effectiveness' of schools or departments are empty unless it is clear what aims are being effectively achieved or what values successfully embodied. Judgements of 'strengths' and 'weaknesses' in schools carry no weight with the parties to the inspection enterprise unless they are in broad agreement on the aims of the activities being inspected and on the contribution of aspects of schools to those aims. 'Value for money' means little without an explicit indication of what is to be valued and what is to count as resources devoted to the pursuit of what is to be valued.

Old-style HMI inspections, as described by Thomas (2001), avoided *in part* the problem of how to make qualitative judgements in the absence of explicit aims and values by evaluating how well individual schools were pursuing *their own* aims and values. However, it has to be acknowledged that such aims were often unclear, indeterminate and rhetorical, rather than informative of practice. Also in asking themselves 'Was what was intended sufficient?' HMI were able to smuggle their own implicit values and aims into the inspection process and into the judgements they made about practices in individual schools. Neither old-style or new-style inspection have successfully addressed the issue of underlying aims and values.

Any national inspection system requires clarity about its own aims and how they relate to the aims and values informing the national system of education. Ofsted needs to clarify the nature of inspection in relation to the kinds of aims and values embodied in the National Curriculum handbooks or whatever replaces them, so as to make the aims of English schooling even more explicit. If the inspection process is not informed by these kinds of aims and values, then individual inspectors will inevitably invest their judgements with implicit aims and values of their own, which may in some respects run counter to those of the educational system itself.

A liberal, democratic society needs *explicit* aims and values, building on those embodied in the National Curriculum handbooks. It also needs a national system of inspection which respects, values, embodies and celebrates those same values and aims.

3
The language of inspection

While introducing some semi-technical phrases of its own , eg. 'schools in need of special measures' or 'schools with serious weaknesses', Ofsted uses everyday English in which to express its findings and judgements. It requires that the reports its inspectors publish should:

> be clear to all its readers, governors, parents, professionals and the public at large...use everyday language, not educational jargon, and be grammatically correct...use telling examples drawn from the evidence base [of the inspection] to make generalisations understandable and to illustrate what is meant by 'good' or 'poor'; employ words and phrases that enliven the report and convey the individual character of the school. (Ofsted 1999b, p. 145)

These are admirable sentiments. Putting aside the impossibility of ensuring clarity to *all* the report's readers (presumably irrespective of their prior knowledge , understanding or experience of schools) how possible is it for reports written in 'everyday' English to be clear, unambiguous and free from the possibility of subtly diverse interpretation?

Educational activities cannot be described or analysed in terms of mathematical formulae. They cannot be appraised using the language, constructs or methodology of the physical sciences. Teaching is not like theoretical physics or even applied mechanics. Pupils observed on inspections are not the equivalent of gases being heated or levers being applied. Still less are they like numbers or algebraic expressions being manipulated. The high (but far from absolute) degree of clarity and precision of description or analysis achieved by physicists is just not possible in education. It is not that sort of activity.

The 'everyday' language available to Ofsted inspectors is potentially extremely flexible, rich and subtle (though in practice the constraints placed on them by Ofsted's monitoring processes lead too often to rigid, formulaic, impoverished and simplistic writing). But it is *inevitably* shot through with ambiguities, imprecision and the possibility of being differently interpreted when it attempts to describe, analyse, interpret or evaluate educational phenomena, not just because of the nature of the phenomena but because of the nature of 'everyday' language itself.

Take just one example, drawn from Ofsted's criteria for judging the quality of teaching:

> inspectors should consider the extent to which teachers challenge and inspire pupils, expecting the most of them, so as to deepen their knowledge and understanding. (Ofsted 1999b, p. 46)

The verb 'to challenge' has a number of meanings: 'invite to take part in ...; invite to prove or justify something; dispute, deny; stretch, stimulate' (Concise Oxford Dictionary, 1995). In relation to any one meaning language users (including inspectors) will have somewhat different views of what constitutes 'challenge', based on their previous experience, knowledge, understanding, values and beliefs. What one inspector may judge as an example of 'challenge', another may judge as an example of 'mismatch' if some of the pupils fail to engage in the activity. Also pupils may well differ from inspectors in their perceptions of what constitutes 'challenge'. Are inspectors reporting their own perceptions, or pupils' perceptions (as they perceive them)?

Likewise, consider 'inspire' ('stimulate or arouse . . .; animate(a person) with feeling; instil (a feeling) into a person; create (a feeling) in a person; prompt, give rise to': Concise Oxford Dictionary, 1995). What one inspector may find 'inspiring' another may find 'pedestrian', depending on his or her previous experience, knowledge, understanding etc. Again pupils in the lesson or lessons where the teaching takes place may differ from inspectors about whether it is 'inspiring'. Whose perceptions are being reported?

Similarly, language users, whether inspectors, teachers or pupils, will differ, sometimes subtly, in their interpretations of what 'expecting the most of' means and whether a particular teaching episode involves 'expecting the most of pupils'. Again what does 'deepen their knowledge and understanding' mean, to whom and in what context?

Such points could be made in relation to all Ofsted's inspection criteria. The attempt made in the Handbooks of Inspection to explain how these criteria are to be used fails to do justice to the nature of the language in which the criteria are expressed and the way that language works.

The point of all this is *not* to argue that Ofsted inspectors should use a technical language, as free as possible from diverse meanings or interpretations. They could not, even if they were required to. The nature of educational phenomena precludes such a language. Ofsted does *indeed* need to report in 'everyday' terms if it is to communicate reasonably effectively (note the qualification!) with readers of its reports but inspectors and those who read their reports need to appreciate the imprecise nature of the language used in reporting, the inevitable variety of interpretations that will be placed on what is reported and the likelihood of teachers and others acting on report findings in ways that are not fully congruent with inspectors' intentions.

Appreciation of the language of Ofsted reports should also warn readers, especially teachers and policy-makers, about the danger of treating inspection judgements as more definitive or authoritative than they can possibly be. Depending on the aspect being reported upon, the person doing the inspecting, the inspection methods being used and the language which is employed, the reliability of inspection judgements varies. At their best they are well-grounded professional judgements, inevitably subjective to a degree, and inevitably expressed in a language far less precise than the language of mathematics or the physical sciences. When given by people whose authority is respected their value can be considerable in informing educational policy and practice.

4
The inspection of standards

As I indicated earlier, the inspection of educational standards is central to inspection under the School Inspections Act of 1996. 'Standards' feature prominently in all Ofsted documentation and reports. For example, the schedule to which all Ofsted inspections have to adhere (Ofsted 1999a, p. 34) highlights as one of its first major sections:

> How high are standards?
> 2.1: The school's results and achievements
> 2.2: Pupils' attitudes, values and personal development

Neither the School Inspections Act nor the Ofsted Inspection framework (Ofsted 1999) defines what is meant by 'standards'. The nearest to an official definition comes in the inspection handbooks:

> In this guidance we use the term *standards* to denote the educational attainment of pupils in relation to some clear benchmark, such as National Curriculum levels, or descriptions, at the end of a Key Stage. 'High' standards, for example, means

that a higher proportion of pupils at a particular age are succeeding at or beyond the level set than in the majority of schools. We also use standards in connection with other less measurable but broadly understood characteristics such as attitudes and behaviour. (Ofsted 1999b, p. 23)

This usage runs counter to Pring's analysis of the concept. Pring (1992, p. 20) characterises standards as 'bench marks ... criteria whereby one assesses or evaluates the quality of a particular activity or process. And that quality must depend upon the identification of the purpose of the activity – upon the values that are embodied within it'.

In its usage Ofsted *does not* distinguish between the standards by which an educational activity or performance is to be evaluated and how far the performance itself meets those standards. Ofsted's usage is related to performance only. Its inspection *judgements* say nothing about the nature of the standards being inspected, only about how far schools' or pupils' performance meets them. The nature of the standards is presupposed; they are not discussed or seen as contentious by Ofsted, yet if Pring's analysis is accepted they are dependent on values and therefore potentially contentious.

Standards

The standards of academic attainment presupposed by Ofsted are those embodied in National Curriculum level descriptions and GCSE and A/AS level grade descriptors. Take those National Curriculum level descriptions. What is their basis? How have they been derived? The procedural answer is that they originated a decade ago in the deliberations of government-appointed subject working parties, were developed in their current form following the Dearing Review in the mid-1990s and were revised for Curriculum 2000 by officials and working parties of the Qualifications and Curriculum Authority following 'consultation' with teachers and other interested parties. They have not been derived as a result of a review of the research literature into how children learn particular aspects of the curriculum; they have not been derived from a philosophical analysis of the structure of particular bodies of knowledge. The level descriptions have been derived pragmatically from a consideration of 'good practice' (value-laden by definition – as if good practice wore its credentials on its face!) and from the beliefs, practices and assumptions of officials and working party members, and have been ordered on a commonsense basis in terms of increasing apparent complexity.

In the real world where decisions need to be taken quickly on timescales derived from political rather than educational imperatives and where relevant psychological research findings or epistemological analyses are not often readily available, such pragmatism is unavoidable. But the arbitrary and potentially contentious basis of these level or grade descriptions needs to be borne in mind when interpreting and considering inspection findings of any school's performance related to them. Nowhere in Ofsted documentation is there any acknowledgement of the arbitrary nature of the level or grade descriptions and of the standards of attainment based on them which it reports.

There is a second feature of level or grade descriptions which limits their use by Ofsted inspectors in making judgements of standards. This is a particular example of a general point made earlier about the language of inspection. Level or grade descriptions are inevitably subject to subtly different interpretations by those using them. As Davis (1999) argues, 'much National Curriculum language is intended to capture knowledge of a general and sometimes abstract character' but 'cannot be used consistently by a range of users in a diversity of contexts'. Frater (1999) illustrates the same point graphically in relation to English level descriptions, noting that 'the descriptions remain profoundly indeterminate. The crucial Level 4 for writing is a clear case in point'. He cites QCA/DfEE 1999a:

Pupils' writing in a range of forms is lively and thoughtful. Ideas are often sustained and developed in interesting ways and organised appropriately for the purpose of the reader. Vocabulary choices are often adventurous and used for effect. Pupils are beginning to use grammatically complex sentences, extending meaning. Spelling, including that of polysyllabic words that conform to regular patterns, is generally accurate ...

Frater comments: *'A range, lively, thoughtful, often sustained, interesting, appropriately adventurous, generally accurate, beginning to use* - each is open to wide interpretation. Placing such value-laden terms at the heart of a level description blunts and softens exactly those hard edges that criterion-referencing was invented to provide'.

Personally I would add *'should* also soften inspection judgements made in relation to those level descriptions'. This does not mean that inspectors cannot, or should not, make judgements in relation to level or grade descriptions but that they can do so only in a rough-and-ready, tentative way – a way which does not rest on fine-grained judgement and which can properly be challenged by teachers holding different interpretations.

Again, parallel to the general points made earlier about the language of inspection, inspectors will not only interpret level or grade descriptions in subtly different ways but may also differ in their interpretation of whether a particular piece of written work, oral contribution, physical demonstration or artefact , which they observe in a classroom, exemplifies fully or partially an aspect of a particular level or grade description. To take an example from the Frater quotation above, vocabulary which one inspector judges to be 'adventuresome' may be interpreted by another as 'bizarre' or 'pretentious'. Spelling which one inspector judges and reports as 'generally accurate' may be judged and reported by another as 'unsatisfactory in certain respects'. In classrooms the 'level' at which pupils are working is not obvious or clear-cut either in the case of individuals or, even more so, in relation to the class as a whole. Pupils do not come wearing level descriptions on their sleeves. Judgements (inevitably subjective and imprecise to a degree) have to be made not only about whether a particular piece of work, a performance or an activity corresponds to a particular level or grade but also about how many such pieces of work have to be observed before an inspector can be reasonably certain that work at a particular level is being consistently achieved and is representative of pupils' general level of performance. Ofsted, however, fails to recognise the inevitable imperfections in the judgements its inspectors report and fails to accept that others may properly contest those judgements.

Performance in relation to standards

In assessing schools' and pupils' *performance* in relation to the standards embodied in National Curriculum level descriptions or GCSE and A/AS level grade descriptors inspectors have to rely on two major sources of evidence: performance data and observations of work seen in school.

Performance data

In Ofsted inspection reports standards expressed in terms of performance data are treated as unproblematic. There is no hint that they are other than definitive, objective *measures* of performance made in relation to commonly agreed and interpreted criteria. Ofsted's uncritical reporting of performance data belies the fact that there are controversies over whether:

(a) it is possible to *measure* (as opposed to *appraise*) performance in relation to the kinds of standards embodied in National Curriculum level descriptions and GCSE and A/AS level descriptors;

(b) it is possible through testing to assess 'connected' knowledge and understanding (as opposed to the 'thin' knowledge required to answer test questions);[4]

(c) all subjects or just a 'core' should be tested or examined;

(d) the most important aspects of particular subjects are, or can be, subject to testing or examining;

(e) the particular tests or examining methods used can reliably and validly assess performance in relation to particular level descriptions or grade descriptors;

(f) the particular tests and examinations can be marked, and the results reported, fairly and consistently;

(g) the results of different tests and examinations can be compared over time.

There are controversies too over the appropriateness of Ofsted's grading and reporting of schools' performance in particular subjects on the basis of aggregated pupil test data and over how far it is possible to compare schools' performance with so-called 'similar' schools (a process termed 'benchmarking', a particularly inappropriate term given its connotations of precision and accuracy and its application in contexts where neither of these qualities is possible). Both of these are prominent features of Ofsted inspection reports. The notion of 'similarity' is especially problematic given the complexity and particularity of individual schools and especially contentious given the high status accorded to such published comparisons. [5]

Inspectors' evaluation of standards

Inspectors are also required to evaluate and report what pupils know, understand and can do and have to assess how well they are achieving. First-hand inspection evidence is to be used to provide 'the current picture of what pupils, including different groups of pupils, are doing well or not so well, and how effectively they are learning' (Ofsted 1999b, p. 23).

That evidence is to be obtained in a variety of ways – through, for example, observing and talking to pupils, analysing the work they have produced, looking at records of attainment, or examining school portfolios of 'levelled' work. The judgements of standards are to be explicitly related to National Curriculum descriptions or GCSE and A/AS grade descriptors. In primary school inspections, for instance, inspectors are instructed to

> bring all of your evidence together so that you can make an overall judgement. You will need to estimate the proportion of pupils who are on course to achieve or exceed the expected goals by the end of the Reception Year, or the expected levels or end of each Key Stage descriptors in the National Curriculum at 7 or 11. Then you are in a position to judge how high standards are. (Ofsted 1999b, p. 33)

Setting aside the contentious issue of how well equipped *anyone* is to offer predictions of the sort required on the basis of limited evidence gathered over a short time-scale, the difficulties of interpreting level descriptions, reliably identifying exemplifications of them and establishing how representative they are of pupils' performance generally, discussed earlier in this chapter, are side-stepped entirely. Ofsted does not explicitly recognise the major problems posed by the use of level or grade descriptors as a way of assessing standards attained by pupils or how well they are achieving.

The question of whether inspectors can possibly take account of the progress pupils have made in determining how well they are achieving depends in part on how far judgements can be made about pupils' learning, both in lessons and over time – issues I discuss in later sections of this pamphlet (pp. 28 - 31, below).

Reporting standards

It is clear that Ofsted gives priority to the reporting of performance data, rather than inspectors' judgements, in order to answer the question 'How high are standards?' In the summary report for parents published after an inspection inspectors are required to complete a table headed STANDARDS to show results at the end of the highest applicable Key Stage. They then have to provide a brief interpretation of the results and evaluate the strengths and weaknesses of the school's performance, trends over time and progress towards its targets (these being expressed in terms of test data) and *only then* assess standards of work seen during the inspection and how well pupils achieve. The table provides grades for each subject or aspect tested, based on Ofsted's own analysis (conducted centrally) of the school's test results. Inspectors are not allowed substantially to change these gradings based on their own judgement of standards without first obtaining Ofsted's permission. Again, when writing the subject sections of full inspection reports inspectors are expected to begin with an analysis of performance data (provided centrally by Ofsted) and an interpretation of the school's performance in national tests and examinations where these are applicable (mathematics, English and science in the case of primary schools).

The emphasis on test data as measures of standards is reinforced in Ofsted's Annual Reports (1999c, 2000a, 2001) where in the sections for primary and secondary schools headed 'Standards achieved' Ofsted *only* reports standards in terms of Key Stage test data and GCSE data, which it claims 'provide a quantitative measure of the national level of pupils' attainment' (Ofsted 2001, p. 89). Ofsted inspectors' judgements of standards are not aggregated nationally to set alongside the test data.

The 'explanation' provided for this absence[6] is unconvincing; it would be very instructive to be able to compare, if only in a rough-and-ready way, inspectors' judgements nationally of how well in general pupils are achieving in relation to national standards (as embodied in level or grade descriptions) with their performance in national tests and examinations which purportedly *measure* pupils' attainment in relation to aspects (though *only* aspects) of those same level or grade descriptions. Why does Ofsted not provide that comparison? Is it because there are marked discrepancies between the two sets of data? Is it because Ofsted tacitly acknowledges the impossibility of judging standards validly and reliably against level or grade descriptions but cannot acknowledge that publicly without appearing to undermine the Ofsted inspection process?

In reporting standards Ofsted adheres to the letter of the 1996 School Inspections Act: it does report on the educational standards achieved in schools. But *does* it adhere to the spirit of that Act? The standards emphasised in individual school inspection reports and in the recent Annual Reports issued by Ofsted are primarily those determined by the devisers of national tests and examinations and by those officials who centrally decide *how the level of performance required for each individual level description to be reached is determined.* Who are these unseen determiners of standards? What authority do they have? What procedures do they use? How are these scrutinised and by whom? How valid and reliable are they? These arbiters of what constitutes 'standards' as reported in Ofsted inspections are neither readily identifiable nor accountable. In a very real sense Ofsted is in danger of breaching the statutory basis on which it was established (see p. 8) In the testable and examinable subjects (presumably those that really matter in Ofsted's and the government's eyes?) Ofsted subordinates the professional expertise of its registered and team inspectors to the expertise of test developers in detemining 'standards'. Does it *distrust* its inspectors' judgement?

5
The inspection of teaching and learning

The 1996 School Inspections Act requires inspectors to report on the quality of education provided by schools. The Ofsted inspection framework highlights as its third major section 'How well are pupils taught?' in which we find the following:

> Inspectors must evaluate and report on:
> * the quality of teaching, judged in terms of its impact on pupils' learning and what makes it successful or not. (Ofsted 1999b, p. 46)

Although philosophers of education dispute the tightness of the logical connection between teaching and learning (see Winch and Gingell 1999), Ofsted is in no doubt as to the tightness of that connection.

> The effectiveness of teaching and the consequent rate, breadth, depth and consolidation of pupils' learning are intrinsically connected. It is the skill of rigorous and perceptive inspection to find, illustrate and evaluate the links between the two. (Ofsted 1999b p. 47)

In offering guidance to its inspectors Ofsted discusses learning first, 'in order to stress the importance of evaluating teaching through its impact' (Ofsted 1999b, p. 52).

Learning

As Winch and Gingell (1999, p. 132) point out:

> Following Ryle (1949) one can distinguish between two senses of a concept like *learning*. The first is the *task* sense; when I say that I am learning German, I mean that I do not yet grasp the language, but the grasping of German is what I am undertaking. When, on the other hand, I say that I have learned German, I am speaking in the *achievement* sense; I have succeeded in learning German. (p. 132)

Ofsted's criteria for judging how well pupils learn and make progress involve *learning* in both senses (my notes in parentheses):

> In determining their judgements, inspectors should consider the extent to which pupils:
> * acquire new knowledge or skills, develop ideas and increase their understanding; [*achievement*]
> * apply intellectual, physical or creative effort in their work; [*task*]
> * are productive and work at a good pace; [*achievement* and *task*]
> * show interest in their work, are able to sustain concentration and think and learn for themselves; [*task* and *achievement*]
> * understand what they are doing, how well they have done and how they can improve. [*achievement*] (Ofsted 1999b, p. 46)

In this pamphlet I distinguish three aspects of learning: two involved in the *task* sense and one in the *achievement* sense. I contend that each has different implications for the possibility of inspection and for the validity and reliability of inspection judgements.

The first *task* aspect relates to whatever internal processes occur in a learner as a result of being taught. The mental strategies, associations or whatever that are involved in that act are unobservable to an inspector (though their neurological basis may be observable to a neurologist using sophisticated equipment!). Inspectors may be able to pick up some clues as to this internal processing through for example talking to pupils, observing their overt behavior or examining their 'working out' of problems on paper or on a computer screen. But such evidence is indirect, partial and difficult to collect during the hectic process of inspection. To all intents and purposes inspection cannot 'get at' whatever internal processes of learning are involved in any *task* of learning.

The second *task* aspect relates to pupils' observable responses to the act of teaching. Are they working at a good pace? Are they interested in the work? Are they concentrating? Are they contributing to the lesson? These are some of the aspects Ofsted inspectors are alerted to when required to make judgements of how well pupils learn. Two points are pertinent here. First, none of these – interest, concentration, hard work, active contribution – are *necessarily* indicative of learning taking place. A pupil, for example, might exhibit all those qualities but simply be revising what he or she already knows. Again a pupil may be feigning these qualities in order to impress the teacher or the inspector. Nevertheless it seems likely, though not certain, that when all or most of these qualities are in evidence, learning of some kind or other is going on. Secondly, there is bound to be an element of invalidity or unreliability when pupils' observable responses are being evaluated. Inspectors may be misled by pupils' apparent behaviour. They are likely to vary somewhat in their interpretation of what constitutes 'a good pace', 'sustained concentration', etc. But with appropriate training, experience and discussion among inspectors it should be possible for their judgements on these aspects to be broadly harmonised and a reasonable degree of validity and reliability of judgment secured.

Ofsted also requires inspectors to evaluate learning in the *achievement* sense. Are the pupils acquiring new knowledge, skills and understanding, including knowledge that is connected to, or applicable in, a range of contexts (Davis's 'connected knowledge', 1999)? Do they understand what they are doing? Have the pupils actually learned something?

But how feasible is it to expect inspectors to be able to make such judgements? Evaluating how well pupils have learned in a lesson involves at least three sets of judgements: (a) judgements of pupils' knowledge, understanding or skills which they 'bring' to the lesson; (b) judgements of the knowledge, understanding and skills they 'take away' at the conclusion of a lesson; and (c) criteria for determining the worthwhileness or otherwise of whatever changes have been detected by inspectors. Except in a minority of cases involving, for example, the learning of very specific physical skills which pupils could not perform at the beginning of a session, or the learning of factual information in science which pupils did not know when tested or closely questioned at the start of the lesson, Ofsted inspectors in their visits to classes do not have, and cannot possibly gain, the *detailed* knowledge of either (a) or (b) and therefore cannot gauge the degree of change in pupils' knowledge, skills or understanding as a result of an act of teaching. Neither can Ofsted provide them with clear and commonly agreed and interpreted criteria for helping them to evaluate whether any change (if it can be identified) means improvement. Of course it is assumed that most pupils do learn something new in most lessons but this is not, except in the minority of cases mentioned above, detectable to any significant degree through observation or brief discussion with pupils by inspectors. It might be possible to evaluate learning in some depth if inspectors had the time to question what they judge to be an appropriate sample of pupils before and after a lesson and to take account of their oral, written and other responses to the teacher. But such circumstances rarely obtain in an Ofsted inspection, nor does Ofsted require such close, in-depth questioning. Davis (1999, p. 36) concurs:

If the lesson aspires to develop children's 'connected' understanding, this cannot be assessed by means of the limited evidence available to the most perceptive of inspectors. It would be difficult even to check whether just one pupil had learned in this rich fashion as a result of the teaching observed.

In the great majority of lessons it is not possible for inspectors to evaluate how well pupils learn in the *achievement* sense.[7] The evidence is simply not available for them to make an evaluative judgement. In the limited number of cases where it is possible, this learning is of a relatively unsophisticated kind - not the 'connected' knowledge to which Davis (1999) refers. In such circumstances inspectors may, again, vary in their judgments of the adequacy or quality of the learning being demonstrated but, as with the aspect above, steps can be taken to harmonise judgements to ensure a reasonable degree of validity and reliability.

It might be argued that if inspection cannot assess the quality and extent of much of pupils' learning, then it can, and should, be replaced by the use of assessment instruments which can *measure* pupils' learning. This, however, sidesteps a large number of practical and logical problems concerned with the use of assessment instruments such as tests and examinations (see pp. 22 - 3). However, it can still be argued that inspection has an important role to play in evaluating some of the *task* senses of teaching and learning (see pp. 29 and 34-5) and in exploring how these may contribute to pupils' achievement, assuming for sake of argument this *can* be ascertained through assessment instruments. On this argument inspection can provide pointers as to why in a particular school pupils' achievement is as it is, and can use that understanding to help teachers improve achievement still further or to improve pupils' achievement in other comparable contexts.

Teaching

As with *learning* I distinguish between two senses of *teaching*. To say 'I taught aspects of place value to children in Year 3' could mean I was *attempting* to teach place value (*the task sense*) without implying that I was successful or not in the venture, or it could mean that I was successful in teaching those aspects to that particular group of pupils (the *achievement* sense). Ofsted's criteria for judging how well teachers teach involve *teaching* in both senses:

In determining their judgements, inspectors should consider the extent to which teachers:

- show good subject knowledge and understanding in the way they present and discuss their subject [*task*]

- are technically competent in teaching phonics and other basic skills [*task*]

- plan effectively, setting clear objectives that pupils understand [*task*]

- challenge and inspire their pupils, expecting the most of them, so as to deepen their knowledge and understanding [*task* and *achievement*]

- use methods which enable all pupils to learn effectively [*task* and *achievement*]

- manage pupils well and insist on high standards of behaviour [*task*]

- use time, support staff and other resources effectively [*task*]

- assess pupils' work thoroughly and use assessments to help and encourage pupils to overcome difficulties [*task* and *achievement*]

- use homework effectively to reinforce and/or extend what is learned in school [*task* and *achievement*] (Ofsted 1999, p. 46)

It should be noted that as worded these criteria are Ofsted's attempt to characterise *good* or *effective* teaching hence the use of words such as 'good', 'effectively', 'thoroughly' and 'well'. Such adjectives and adverbs raise the issue of what constitutes 'effectiveness', 'thoroughness' or 'good quality' – which brings into play a range of implicit values. Stripped of such adjectives and adverbs the criteria might plausibly be seen as useful but minimal criteria for judging whether or not someone is actually teaching (Winch 1996).

In line with the Ofsted inspection schedule to which they have to adhere, inspectors' judgements about the quality of teaching refer to one or more of three senses of teaching: one concerned with teaching in the *achievement* sense and two in terms of the *task* sense. However, in inspection reports summary judgments such as 'In Key Stage 2 the quality of teaching was good, while in Key Stage 1 it was satisfactory' do not make it clear which sense or senses are being referred to. Again, when summarising inspectors' judgements to the effect, for example, that in primary schools 'The overall improvement in the quality of teaching reported in last year's Annual Report has continued' (Ofsted 2001, p. 26), Ofsted's Annual Reports do not distinguish between the three senses of 'good' or 'effective' teaching which underpin those judgements. I contend that as with *learning* each sense of teaching has different implications for the possibility of inspection and for the validity and reliability of inspection judgements.

The judgements made by Ofsted inspectors in answering the question 'How well are pupils taught?' involve criteria related to the *effectiveness* of the teaching in bringing about learning. For example, are teachers using methods to enable children to learn effectively? Are they deepening pupils' knowledge and understanding? These are judgements about teaching in the *achievement* sense. They are based on the reasonable assumption that in most cases teaching leads to learning of some kind. However, in order to make a judgement of the effectiveness of the teaching in bringing about learning inspectors have to be in a position to gather reliable evidence of the learning that has been fostered by the teaching observed in particular lessons. If my arguments advanced in relation to the evaluation of learning in the *achievement* sense (pp. 30 - 1) are accepted, then such judgements are simply not possible except in the minority of cases outlined there. Only in those cases is it possible to secure a reasonable degree of validity and reliability in judgements. However, to repeat a point made earlier, in the great majority of lessons the evidence needed to make valid, reliable judgements about the effectiveness of teaching in bringing about learning is just not available.This is not a technical problem which Ofsted could easily solve by modifying its procedures; it would require a very different, time-consuming, labour-intensive research-oriented methodology based on in-depth interviewing of pupils before and after lessons. Even then it would be impossible to determine with certainty whether a particular episode of teaching or a particular componment within that act of teaching had actually *caused* the learning to occur.

There is a second sense underlying the Ofsted criteria for judging teaching. This *task* sense refers to the way in which lessons are conducted. 'Good' lessons are those where, for example, the work is carefully planned; the lesson has a clear structure; teaching points are made cogently; clear routines are in operation; resources are available when required; pupils are managed well; time and support staff are used appropriately, etc. It seems reasonable to argue that the presence of such features is likely to enhance the possibility of the teaching leading to the intended learning but their presence does not guarantee learning in the *achievement* sense. However such features are important and they are observable. Inspectors can gain sufficient evidence to be able to make and justify judgements of teaching quality in this *task* sense. Of course even here there is likely to be an element of unreliability of judgements between inspectors but such unreliability can be kept within acceptable limits through appropriate guidance by Ofsted and by discussion and moderation by inspectors themselves.

There is, however, a second *task* sense of teaching which, in my view, is almost certainly influencing inspectors' judgements of quality in some areas of the curriculum, especially in primary schools and increasingly in Key Stage 3 in secondary schools. As a result of the introduction of the Literacy and Numeracy Strategies there are now national prescriptions concerned with such aspects of teaching as the structure of lessons, the forms of grouping to be employed and the nature of plenary sessions. These have, rightly or wrongly, achieved virtually canonical status among inspectors – they provide the model of how numeracy and literacy lessons ought to be conducted. 'Good' lessons are those that conform to the national prescriptions; 'good' teaching employs the kinds of teaching methods in the kinds of combinations and over the time scales advocated in the national strategies. Such features are observable and reportable. Because of the detailed prescription provided in the literacy and numeracy documentation and because of the training undertaken by both teachers and inspectors there is likely to be less room for differences in interpretation about the extent and quality of the implementation of these teaching methods by inspectors compared with their judgements about the general features involved in the first *task* sense of teaching discussed in the previous paragraph. I think it is possible to provide valid, reliable inspection judgements about the extent to which teachers' practice conforms to the accepted model of 'good' teaching enshrined in the national strategies. But 'good' in this sense does not *necessarily* mean 'good' in the sense of enhancing children's learning.

It is instructive to consider what lies behind Ofsted's firm contention in its 1998-9 Annual Report that 'English primary schools have continued to improve. There is better teaching and , as a consequence, pupils are learning more' (Ofsted 2000a, p. 23). If my arguments in this pamphlet are accepted, Ofsted *cannot* have evidence of a direct link between the teaching observed by its inspectors and the learning of pupils in the schools inspected. Ofsted may, however, have some reasonably reliable evidence that the conduct of lessons (in the first *task* sense) has improved. But what is more likely to lie behind the assertion is inspectors' accumulation of evidence that the accepted model of 'good' teaching advocated in the national strategies has increasingly been observed on Ofsted inspections, themselves heavily biased towards the inspection of numeracy and literacy. How far it characterises teachers' practice outside the period of inspections, and how far teachers have accepted the model as the most appropriate way of teaching are problematic and contentious.

6
More limitations of inspection

Part of my purpose in writing this pamphlet is to establish some of the limitations of the Ofsted inspection process and to argue that Ofsted claims too much for its inspection methodology and its outcomes.[8] The previous section has exposed some of these limitations as they apply to teaching and learning. Ofsted employs a large number of other concepts which need to be subject to scrutiny but in this section I discuss only two of them briefly. Both *progress* and *improvement* are central to the Ofsted inspection process, especially now that schools are being inspected for the second time and judgements about progress and improvement *seem* possible. However, I argue that their use both in school inspection reports and in Ofsted Annual Reports is flawed.

Progress

In the inspection framework issued in 1995 *progress* featured very prominently. The Handbook for the Inspection of Primary and Nursery Schools made it clear in a major section entitled 'Attainment and Progress' that 'The main priorities of inspection are to *assess* what pupils know, understand and can do – that it to say, their attainment; and to *evaluate* their progress' (Ofsted 1995, p. 55). It went on to stress that judging progress

calls on inspectors to evaluate a complex set of evidence ranging from progress observed in lessons (i.e. 'what did pupils learn?'), to progress made over longer periods of time such as from one stage of schooling to the next. Progress is defined as gains in knowledge, understanding and skill. (p. 55)

As a result of these requirements, along with the requirement to grade the quality of progress made in each lesson, all school inspection reports issued between 1995 and 1999 referred to the progress made by pupils over Key Stages and in lessons. In addition Ofsted Annual Reports made copious references to the progress pupils were believed to have made. The following assertion, taken from the 1997/98 Annual Report (Ofsted 1999c), is typical of many:

In both Key Stage 1 and Key Stage 2 inspectors report that pupils generally make greater gains in knowledge, understanding and skills than in previous years. In every year group more lessons were seen this year where progress was good or very good and fewer where it was unsatisfactory. (p. 21)

In the most recent inspection framework issued in 1999 *progress* receives a far less prominent place (though, interestingly, no explanation of its 'demotion' has been offered by Ofsted). It no longer features as part of a major heading and gradings of progress in lessons are no longer required. It does, however, still feature in the section 'How well are pupils taught?', though far less prominently than judgements of the quality of teaching. Here, as indicated earlier in the pamphlet, inspectors have to evaluate and report on how well pupils learn and make progress. But how possible it is for inspectors to make and report judgements of progress, either within individual lessons or over longer periods of time?

I do not need to rehearse again the arguments already made (pp. 30 - 1 and 33 - 4) to the effect that except in a minority of cases it is impossible for inspectors to make reasonably reliable and valid judgements of progress (i.e. 'gains in knowledge, understanding and skill') in individual lessons. It is a fact, however, that between 1995 and 1999 inspectors did *try* to judge and report upon progress within lessons but their 'judgements' could have been inferences only – presumably based on their evaluation of the quality of teaching in the first *task* sense (p. 34) and their evaluation of the quality of pupils' observable responses to the teaching (the second *task* aspect of learning: see p. 39). No attempt was made to establish the degree of reliability of these potentially fallible inferences by a methodology independent of Ofsted inspection.

Equally problematic are judgements of progress made over longer periods of time based on scrutiny of work from pupils in different year groups. When required to make judgements of the progress children make over the course of a Key Stage in a particular school inspectors usually have to scrutinise samples of the work of different year groups of pupils collected in the same school year, not extensive samples of work of the same year group of children collected over the whole period of a Key Stage. In such scrutiny like is not being compared with like: the populations whose work is being sampled and examined are bound to vary in a variety of ways. Even when it is possible to compare the work of the same year group over time other factors could account for changes in the quality of work scrutinised, some of which would not have been under the direct influence of the school (such as pupil turnover). Of those which are subject to the school's influence some or all might no longer apply at the time of the inspection. Such scrutiny of pupils' work, usually conducted hurriedly and superficially due to the inevitable time constraints of an inspection, is an inadequate basis for judging the progress children make over time.

All of this throws doubt on the weight Ofsted has placed, and still to some extent places, on judgements of progress made in individual schools and on the overall judgements of progress copiously referenced in its Annual Reports (e.g. Ofsted 1999c, 2000a).

Improvement

The latest inspection framework issued with effect from January 2000 makes much of the concept of *improvement*. Under the title 'What sort of school is it?' the very first section of the guidance on using the 'Evaluation Schedule' (Ofsted 1999b, p. 10) states that Inspectors must report on the characteristics of the school and evaluate and summarise:

- the effectiveness of the school...
- the main strengths and weaknesses of the school
- the extent to which the school has improved, or not, since the last inspection

Furthermore Inspectors should relate their findings 'to the specific nature of the school and its pupils' *(ibid)*.

All school inspection reports now contain judgements as to how far the school on its second inspection has improved relative to its first and whether that degree of improvement has been sufficient. Such judgements are usually expressed authoritatively, without any degree of tentativeness. Likewise the most recent Annual Report makes confident assertions that 'The improvement in primary education has continued ... There have been improvements in leadership and management ... Most schools have made good progress since their previous inspection' (Ofsted 2001, p. 22)

But the use of the concept of *improvement* is highly problematic when applied in this context. To judge validly and reliably the extent of improvement from one inspection to the next requires at least the following: (a) in-depth knowledge of the school at the time of its first inspection; (b) in-depth knowledge of the school at the time of its second; (c) the same criteria of judgement employed on both occasions; (d) the criteria employed in the same way on both occasions; (e) criteria for judging the worthwhileness (or otherwise) of any changes detected. In reality a previously published inspection report, however well written, cannot provide the detail required by (a) in order to be compared with (b). Inspection by exactly the same team on both occasions might provide a reasonably valid and reliable comparison provided inspectors have good memories and plentiful written evidence from the last inspection but such a situation rarely, if ever, obtains. In relation to (c) there have been significant changes to the inspection criteria over time, and changes in the instructions given to inspectors on how to apply them, both of which render comparisons of inspection judgements over time questionable. Ofsted has no way of guaranteeing (d) though its monitoring programmes help ensure some degree of consistency of usage, but this is not the case in every inspection since not all inspections are monitored. In relation to (e) Ofsted does not, indeed cannot, provide inspectors with clear and commonly agreed and interpreted criteria for helping them to evaluate validly and reliably whether change equates to improvement.

It has to be acknowledged that in a very limited way Ofsted is able to document *change*. It can, for example, report that certain features missing in a first inspection (for examples, policies, schemes of work, appraisal arrangements) are present in a second inspection. It can validly report changes in quantitative indicators such as attendance rates or test scores provided the bases on which the data have been collected have remained the same over time. However, whether such changes represent 'improvement' is a value judgement, much more contentious in relation to test scores, say, than in relation to attendance rates. However, even when they can be made, such comments are but a minor contribution to the requirement laid on Ofsted inspectors to 'evaluate and summarise ... the extent to which the school has improved, or not, since the last inspection' (Ofsted 1999b, p. 10).

I contend that any overall judgements about the improvement of a school from one inspection to the next or about the improvement of English schools over time on the basis of aggregated judgments of improvements in individual schools are suspect. Once again, Ofsted promises more than it can reliably deliver.

7
Conclusion: possibilities for inspection

Assuming all or some of the limitations discussed in this pamphlet are valid, where does that leave Ofsted inspection? Should the Ofsted inspection process be modified, radically overhauled or dispensed with altogether? Certainly the limitations imply that the Ofsted process is in need of urgent review in terms of aims and values, the concepts it employs, the way it operationalises them, the methodology it uses and the justifications it offers for its activities and its judgements. The appointment of a new Chief Inspector offers the opportunity for a fundamental review.

This pamphlet is not the place to offer detailed suggestions as to what in particular that review should focus on, how it should be conducted and what its conclusions might be. But in view of the critique offered of the Ofsted process I need to discuss, if only briefly, the issue of the possible uses of inspection as an educational methodology for the purpose of evaluation and accountability

I want to argue that school inspection has a number of uses[9] – more limited than the claims of Ofsted or, for that matter, of 'old-style' HMI inspection but important for all that. These uses depend on the use of first-hand observation and discussion by professionals to interpret complex educational situations and to communicate those interpretations to others with an interest in the outcomes and/or processes of schooling. Some, but not all, of these activities could be undertaken by others such as 'non-educational' researchers or even market research personnel but most could not, since they involve evaluation related to educational aims and values and they require expertise based on knowledge and understanding of schools. They include (in no order of precedence) the use of school inspection to:

(1) check on whether and how far schools are complying with relevant statutory requirements and ascertain and report back to central government any problems or issues arising from attempts to comply (or to avoid compliance);

(2) evaluate and report on observable features of school provision such as the state of repair of the fabric of buildings or the quality and quantity of resources;

(3) evaluate and report on the progress made, and the problems encountered, in introducing particular initiatives;

(4) evaluate and report on the effects of central or local government policies on policy and practice in schools;

(5) collect, report and evaluate the perceptions of interested parties (pupils, teachers, parents, governors) in relation to identified issues;

(6) offer possible explanations of how particular outcomes have been achieved in particular schools and disseminate that information to other schools and interested parties;

(7) offer tentative, broad-brush judgements as to how far individual schools appear to be meeting their own aims and values or the aims and values of school education in England (if these were to be agreed);

(8) offer tentative judgements as to how well lessons are conducted and on pupils' observable responses to teaching;

(9) offer broad, tentative judgements about the quality of pupils' performance in particular subjects compared with those in schools in roughly comparable contexts;

(10) offer inspectors' interpretations of activities they see as a basis for dialogue with those who have been observed and who may have differing interpretations;

(11) validate schools' processes of self-review.

Ofsted *does* and in my view *should* have a future as an organisation involved in observing practice in schools, collecting evidence, making qualitative judgements, evaluating and interpreting complex educational situations, reporting its findings and making observations of the interplay between processes and outcomes. In particular the government needs an agency which can quickly, independently and on the basis of first-hand evidence offer advice on the effects of policy on practice. But Ofsted needs to do so with a clearer and more open acknowledgement of the limitations under which it operates and which affect the authoritativeness of its findings.

Although lacking the apparent authority and comprehensiveness claimed by Ofsted for its inspection process, the importance of the uses of inspection (outlined above) in offering informed interpretations and in influencing educational policy and practice should not be underestimated. However, whether such inspection should be carried out by a modifed Ofsted, by a resurrected H.M. Inspectorate or by some other body is *in part* a political question beyond the scope of this pamphlet.

Acknowledgement

In writing this paper the author has benefited greatly from comments made by Mike Sullivan, Brenda Lofthouse, Norman Thomas HMI (retired), Graham Frater HMI (retired), David Scott HMI (retired), Philip Taylor, Sheila Dainton, Richard Smith, Christopher Winch and Andrew Davis.

Notes

1. For a philosophical discussion of inspection and other instruments of quality assessment and accountability see Winch (1996).

2. For my views on the effects of Ofsted inspection on schools and teachers see Richards (1997a, 1997b, 2000a, 2000b).

3. Other examples of such aims include (DfEE/QCA 1999a, pp. 11-12):
   (a) The school curriculum should develop enjoyment of, and commitment to, learning. . .

   (b) It should equip pupils with the essential learning skills of literacy, numeracy and information and communication technology, and promote an enquiring mind and capacity to think rationally.

   (c) It should encourage pupils to appreciate human aspirations and achievements in aesthetic, scientific, technological and social fields.

   (d) It should develop pupils' knowledge, understanding and appreciation of their own and different beliefs and cultures.

   (e) It should also equip pupils as consumers to make informed judgements and independent decisions and to understand their responsibilities and their rights.

   (f) It should enable pupils to respond positively to opportunities, challenges and responsibilities, to manage risk and to cope with change and adversity.

4. See Davis's argument in his Impact pamphlet *Educational Assessment: a critique of current policy* (1999).

5. The dubious uses of the notion of 'similarity' by Ofsted and other official agencies are cogently criticised in Davis (1999).

6. Ofsted's explanation appears in an annex:

Inspectors make two separate judgements of standards achieved by pupils:

- standards of work seen — emphasising numeracy and literacy and highlighting strengths and weaknesses in what pupils know, understand and can do;

- how well the pupils achieve, taking account of the progress they have made and other relevant factors.

The term 'standards' is used to indicate the educational attainment of pupils in relation to clear benchmarks such as National Curriculum levels. When grading the standards of work seen, inspectors judge whether the proportion of pupils achieving the national expectation is below, broadly in line with or above that which is found nationally. This comparison with norms is a key part of the judgement of standards and provides important information for the school being inspected. However, because the inspection grades for attainment are made in comparison with a national norm, when aggregated nationally they can only produce a distribution about that norm, rather than a measure of the national level of attainment of pupils. In this report, evidence from national tests and examinations is used to provide a quantitative measure of the national level of pupils' attainment. (Ofsted 2001 p. 89)

7. Arguably, it is possible for inspectors to evaluate learning in a negative sense. If the features associated with the first 'task' sense of teaching (p. 34) are not observable, it is probable, but even here not certain, that the learning envisaged by the teacher is not taking place.

8. Its pretentious claims have never been more evident than in its recently published guidance, *Evaluating Educational Inclusion* (2000b), where it requires its inspectors to assess the impossible, i.e. whether *'all* pupils are achieving *as much as they can,* and deriving the *maximum* benefit, according to their *individual* needs, from what the school provides' (my italics). I am grateful to Sheila Dainton for drawing my attention to this requirement. Like her, I believe that this is nonsense.

9. Some of these are discussed in the final chapter of Davis's Impact pamphlet *Educational Assessment: a critique of current policy* (1999)

References

Bramall, S. and White, J. (2000) *Will the new National Curriculum live up to its aims?* Impact No.6, London: Philosophy of Education Society of Great Britain

Davis, A. (1999) *Educational Assessment: a critique of current policy,* Impact No. 1, London: Philosophy of Education Society of Great Britain

Department for Education and Employment (DfEE)/ Qualifications and Curriculum Authority (QCA) (1999a) *The National Curriculum Handbook for Primary Teachers in England,* London: DfEE/QCA

Department for Education and Employment (DfEE)/ Qualifications and Curriculum Authority (QCA) (1999b) *The National Curriculum Handbook for Secondary Teachers in England,* London: DfEE/QCA

Department for Education and Science (1985) *Better Schools,* London: HMSO

Frater, G. (1999) National initiatives for literacy, *Education 3-13, 27:1,* 3-11

Office for Standards in Education (Ofsted) (1995) *Guidance on the Inspection of Nursery and Primary Schools,* London: HMSO

Office for Standards in Education (Ofsted) (1999a) *Inspecting Schools: The Framework,* London: Ofsted

Office for Standards in Education (Ofsted) (1999b) *Handbook for Inspecting Primary and Nursery Schools,* London: HMSO

Office for Standards in Education (Ofsted) (1999c) *Standards and Quality in Education 1997-98: The Annual Report of Her Majesty's Chief Inspector of Schools,* London: HMSO

Office for Standards in Education (2000a) *Standards and Quality in Education 1998-99: The Annual Report of Her Majesty's Chief Inspector of Schools,* London: HMSO

Office for Standards in Education (2000b) *Evaluating Educational Inclusion,* London: Office for Standards in Education

Office for Standards in Education (2001) *Standards and Quality in Education 1999-2000: The Annual Report of Her Majesty's Chief Inspector of Schools,* London: HMSO

Pring, R. (1992) Standards and quality in education, *British Journal of Educational Studies,* 40.1, 4-22

Richards, C. (1997a) The high price of inspection, *The Guardian,* June 3

Richards, C. (1997b) Casualties of inspection, *Education Journal*, November

Richards, C. (2000a) The profession's poultice, *Times Educational Supplement,* December 8

Richards, C. (2000b) Survivors of Inspection, *Education Journal*, November

Ryle, G. (1949) *The Concept of Mind,* London: Hutchinson

Thomas, N. (2001) Assessing schools: quantity is no substitute for quality, in: Richards, C. (Ed.) *Changing English Primary Education: retrospect and prospect,* Stoke-on-Trent: Trentham Books, pp. 57-65

Thompson, D. (ed.) (1995) *The Concise Oxford Dictionary of Current English*, ninth edition, Oxford: Clarendon Press

Winch, C. (1996) *Quality and Education*, Oxford: Blackwell

Winch, C. and Gingell, J. (1999) *Key Concepts in the Philosophy of Education*, London: Routledge

Suggestions for further reading

Centre for the Study of Public Policy and Practice (1999) *The Ofsted System of School Inspection: an independent evaluation*, London: Brunel University

Davis, A. (1998) *The Limits of Educational Assessment*, Oxford: Blackwell

Davis, A. (1999) *Educational Assessment: a critique of current policy*, Impact No. 1 London: Philosophy of Education Society of Great Britain

Frater, G. (1995) *Criteria or Chimera? Standards for assessment and inspection: some problems of definition*, Sheffield: The National Association for the Teaching of English

Gilroy, P. and Wilcox, B. (1977) OFSTED, criteria and the nature of social understanding: a Wittgensteinian critique of the practice of educational judgement, *British Journal of Educational Studies*, 45.1, pp. 22 - 38

National Union of Teachers (2001) *Education Review* 14.2, Inspection and Accountability

Richards, C. (1997) *Primary Education, Standards and Ofsted: towards an authentic conversation*, Occasional Paper, Coventry: Centre for Elementary and Primary Education, University of Warwick

Thomas, N. (2001) Assessing schools: quantity is no substitute for quality, in: *Richards, C. (Ed.) Changing English Primary Education: retrospect and prospect*, Stoke-on-Trent: Trentham Books, pp. 57-65

Wilcox, B. and Gray, J. (1996) *Inspecting Schools: holding schools to account and helping schools to improve*, Buckingham: Open University Press

Winch, C. (1996) *Quality and Education*, Oxford: Blackwell

Topics of forthcoming titles from IMPACT

- Personal, Social and Health Education

- Citizenship Education

- Good Teaching

- Gifted Pupils

- Environmental Education

If you would like to be put on a mailing list for further information about the publication of these pamphlets and about any symposia or other events connected with their launch, please contact:

Sally Armstrong
University College Northampton
Boughton Green Road
Northampton NN2 7AL
Telephone 01604 735500
Fax 01604 713759
Email: sally.armstrong@northampton.ac.uk
or
christopher.winch@northampton.ac.uk

Join the
Philosophy of Education Society of Great Britain
and receive the

Journal of Philosophy of Education

FREE!

Formed in 1964, the Society exists to promote the study, teaching and application of Philosophy of Education. It holds an annual three-day conference as well as local meetings and conferences. Members receive the Journal of Philosophy of Education as part of the benefits of their annual membership.

Membership rates:

(worldwide) £24.00 (£12.00 unwaged; £8.00 non-Western income as determined by the Executive Committee).
Payment by credit card possible (with £2.00 surcharge).

Membership enquiries: please contact
Dr. Colin Wringe
Department of Education
Univesity of Keele
Staffordshire ST5 5BG UK

Email: eda26@educ.keele.ac.uk

JOURNAL OF PHILOSOPHY OF EDUCATION

THE JOURNAL OF THE PHILOSOPHY OF EDUCATION SOCIETY OF GREAT BRITAIN

Edited by PAUL STANDISH

Journal of Philosophy of Education publishes articles representing a wide variety of philosophical traditions. They vary from examination of fundamental philosophical issues in their connection with education, to detailed critical engagement with current educational practice or policy from a philosophical point of view.

The *Journal* aims to promote rigorous thinking on educational matters and to identify and criticise the ideological forces shaping education. Ethical, political, aesthetic and epistemological dimensions of educational theory are amongst those covered.

JOURNAL OF PHILOSOPHY OF EDUCATION ISSN: 0309-8249. VOLUME 35 (2001) CONTAINS 4 ISSUES.

Select✓ BLACKWELL PUBLISHERS' EMAIL UPDATES

WE ARE PLEASED TO ANNOUNCE THE LAUNCH OF OUR NEW EMAIL ALERTING SERVICE. YOU CAN NOW RECEIVE THE TABLES OF CONTENTS OF *JOURNAL OF PHILOSOPHY OF EDUCATION* EMAILED DIRECTLY TO YOUR DESKTOP. UNIQUELY FLEXIBLE, SELECT ALLOWS YOU TO CHOOSE EXACTLY THE INFORMATION YOU NEED. FOR *FREE* UPDATES ON BLACKWELL PUBLISHERS' TITLES SIMPLY VISIT: **HTTP://SELECT.BLACKWELLPUBLISHERS.CO.UK**

✓ SELECT EXACTLY WHAT YOU WANT TO RECEIVE
✓ SELECT CONTENTS TABLES FROM THE JOURNALS OF YOUR CHOICE
✓ SELECT NEWS OF BOOKS AND JOURNALS BY SUBJECT AREA
✓ SELECT WHEN YOUR MESSAGES ARRIVE, RIGHT DOWN TO THE DAY OF THE WEEK

108 COWLEY ROAD, OXFORD OX4 1JF, UK
350 MAIN STREET, MALDEN, MA 02148, USA
JNLINFO@BLACKWELLPUBLISHERS.CO.UK

IB BLACKWELL *Publishers*

VISIT OUR WEBSITE FOR CONTENTS LISTINGS, ABSTRACTS, SAMPLES, AND TO SUBSCRIBE

W W W . B L A C K W E L L P U B . C O M